King Lear

A Shakespeare Story

RETOLD BY ANDREW MATTHEWS
ILLUSTRATED BY TONY ROSS

ORCHARD

For Stephen
A.M.

ORCHARD BOOKS
338 Euston Road, London NW1 3BH
Orchard Books Australia
Hachette Children's Books
Level 17/207 Kent St, Sydney, NSW 2000
First published in Great Britain in 2009
First paperback publication in 2010
This slipcase edition published in 2013
Not for individual resale
Text © Andrew Matthews 2009
Illustrations © Tony Ross 2009
ISBN 978 1 40780 977 9
The rights of Andrew Matthews to be identified as the author and Tony Ross as
the illustrator of this work have been asserted by them in accordance with the
Copyright, Designs and Patents Act, 1988.
A CIP catalogue record for this book is available from the British Library
Printed in China

Orchard Books is a division of Hachette Childrens Books,
an Hachette UK company.
www.hachette.co.uk

Contents

Cast List

King Lear
King of Britain

Cordelia
Lear's daughter

Goneril
Lear's daughter, wife of the
Duke of Albany

Regan
Lear's daughter, wife of the
Duke of Cornwall

Earl of Gloucester

Lear's oldest friend and ally

Edgar

Gloucester's heir

Earl of Kent

Lear's faithful servant

Edmund

Gloucester's illegitimate son

The Scene

Ancient Britain.

Better thou
Hadst not been born than not t'have
pleased me better.

Lear; I.i.

King Lear

In his youth, Lear had won the crown of Britain through his strength, courage and cunning, and he had enjoyed ruling the country. Now he was old. His eyes were dull, his hair white and his face wrinkled.

The aged King addressed the nobles he had summoned to his throne room. "I intend to give up the crown before the strain of ruling becomes too much," he said. "Britain will be divided into three, to be ruled by my daughters. The richest part will be given to the one who loves me most.

Goneril, my eldest child, wife
of Albany – how much
do you love me?"

Goneril had
red hair, and
a haughty
expression.
"I love you
more than
words can say,"
she declared,
"more than
my own life!"

Lear smiled.
"And what does
my second daughter,
Regan, wife of
Cornwall, have to say?"
he demanded.

Regan's golden curls and simpering smile masked her greed and slyness. "My love is greater than Goneril's," she claimed. "My only true pleasure is your happiness."

Lear nodded, and spoke to his youngest daughter, Cordelia. She was being wooed by the King of France, who was present.

"Now, dearest daughter," Lear said affectionately, "what have you to tell me?"

Cordelia's black hair and dark gown emphasised the paleness of her face. She struggled to speak, then blurted out, "Nothing, my lord."

Lear frowned. "Nothing?" he snapped. "If you say nothing, you'll get nothing. Speak again!"

"I'm not like my sisters!" Cordelia cried. "I can't flatter you with empty words. I love you as much as a daughter ought to love her father, no more, no less. That's the truth."

Lear's face flushed dark with fury. "Then let the truth be your only dowry, for you'll get nothing from me!" he hissed. "Goneril and Regan can share your third of the kingdom. Leave my court and my heart. You are no daughter of mine!"

Cordelia lowered her head, and wept silently.

"My power now passes to my two remaining daughters," Lear went on. "I shall keep the title of King, and a company of a 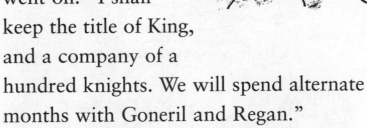 hundred knights. We will spend alternate months with Goneril and Regan."

A stocky, grey-haired man stepped forwards. He was the Earl of Kent, Lear's most trusted and loyal servant. "My lord, have you gone mad?" he spluttered. "Anyone can see how Cordelia loves you. You're making a foolish mistake!"

Rage brought Lear to his feet. His hand trembled as he pointed at Kent. "I banish you!" he screeched. "You have five days to make yourself ready. After that, if you're found anywhere in my kingdom, you will be executed!"

Kent left without saying another word.

Lear spoke to the King of France. "Since my daughter has no dowry, I will understand if you withdraw your marriage offer," he said.

The French King's gaze was fixed on Cordelia. "Cordelia's honesty makes me love her even more," he announced. "I would be honoured to marry her."

"Then take her, with my curse upon her!" growled Lear. "I wish she had never been born."

The old King swept out of the throne room, and the nobles followed him; but Goneril and Regan lingered, whispering together in a shadowy corner.

"The old man is losing his wits," murmured Regan. "He always loved Cordelia best, and now he has left her penniless."

"And even though he has given up the crown, he banished Kent," Goneril pointed out. "I fear he is going to interfere with every decision we make. Our lives will be a misery."

"Then we must do something to stop him," said Regan.

✳ ✳ ✳

When the Earl of Gloucester returned to his castle, the scene he had witnessed in Lear's throne room still burned in his mind.

"My old friend Kent banished!" he muttered to himself. "Lear giving up his throne! What is the world coming to?"

Gloucester was so deep in thought that he almost collided with Edmund, his illegitimate son. For years Edmund had lived secretly abroad, and as far as the nobles at court knew, Gloucester's only child and heir was his son Edgar. The recent death of his wife had made the Earl realise how old he was getting, and he had sent for Edmund, hoping they would get to know each other a little better.

Edmund seemed startled when his
father appeared, and
stuffed a sheet of
paper into the
pocket of his
doublet.

"What's that?"
Gloucester
enquired.

"Nothing!"
said Edmund.

"If it's nothing,
why are you trying
to hide it?" Gloucester said.

"It's a letter from Edgar," Edmund
admitted. "I hid it because I thought it
would upset you."

"Let me see for myself!" Gloucester
insisted.

Edmund obediently handed his father the letter.

"Father grows weaker and more foolish every day," Gloucester read aloud. "Why should we have to wait to enjoy what is rightfully ours? Join forces with me. We can get rid of the old man, and share his fortune. Your brother, Edgar."

Shock turned Gloucester's face grey. "How could my son have written this?" he mumbled. "But the handwriting looks like his!"

"Edmund must have meant it as a test – or a joke," suggested Edmund.

"I'll give him joke!" snarled Gloucester. "I'll have him arrested and imprisoned."

The Earl hurried off down a nearby corridor.

When he was alone, Edmund chuckled. "I knew that forging your handwriting would prove useful, Edgar!" he gloated. "My half-brother is too noble to suspect me of treachery, and my father will believe anything I tell him. Perfect! That will make it easy to take revenge on them for all the years that they ignored me."

✳ ✳ ✳

Instead of leaving Britain, Kent shaved off his hair, disguised himself as a poor man, and managed to get a job as Lear's servant. Before long, Kent noticed that all was not well. Goneril found fault with almost everything that Lear did, and he often lost his temper with her,  suddenly flying into a ranting rage.

One afternoon, Lear was in his private chamber, chatting to his Fool and Kent, when Goneril and Albany came in.

Goneril scowled at her father.

"Why are you frowning, daughter?"
said Lear.

"You didn't care about her frowns
when you were King," the Fool observed.
"Now, I'm better than you. I'm a fool,
but you are nothing."

"I frown because your Fool makes fun of me," said Goneril, "and because your knights do nothing but eat, drink and quarrel with my servants. Since you refuse to do anything about this, I must deal with it myself. Half your knights will be sent away."

Lear concealed his humiliation with sarcasm. "Do you know me?" he said to the Fool and Kent. "I can't be Lear. Goneril would never speak to her father the way she spoke to me. But if I'm not Lear, who am I?"

"Lear's shadow," muttered the Fool.

Lear looked up at the ceiling. "Gods, if Goneril has a child, let it be ungrateful and disobedient, so that she can feel what I am feeling!" he cried. "I'll go to Regan. When she hears how you've treated me, she will tear your face with her nails."

Lear stormed out of the chamber, with the Fool and Kent close behind.

Albany glanced anxiously at his wife. "Is this wise?" he said. "Your father might make trouble between you and Regan."

"I sent Regan a letter, explaining what I intended to do, and she approved," replied Goneril. "My father is no longer King. His tantrums are no more than the squalling of a brat!"

Albany said nothing, but inside he was alarmed at how hardhearted his wife had become.

* * *

Regan and Cornwall were staying as Gloucester's guests. Accompanied by Kent and the Fool, Lear rode to Gloucester's castle. They arrived at dusk. The sky was dark with clouds, and distant thunder rumbled. To Lear's dismay, he was greeted by both Regan and Goneril, as well as

Gloucester, Edmund and Cornwall.

"Regan, how can you bear your sister's company after the way she has insulted me?" Lear whined. "She wants me to give up half my knights."

"I don't see why you need any knights at all," Regan responded. "If you stay with me, you must come alone."

"But I must have knights!" spluttered Lear. "I am King!"

"You *were* King!" Goneril corrected him.

In the sudden glare of a lightning bolt, Lear saw his daughters' cruelty and coldness. The love they had once declared for him was a lie.

The old man clutched
the Fool's arm
for support. "I'll
go mad if I stay
here!" he gasped.
The Fool and Kent
helped Lear remount
his horse as a heavy
rain began to fall.
"Where will you shelter,
my lord?" Gloucester
called out.

"In a ditch for all
I care!" said Regan.
"A good soaking might
bring him to his senses."

Goneril laughed at this
remark, then she, Regan and Cornwall
retreated into the castle.

"It's not natural for children to treat their father so heartlessly," said Gloucester. "There is going to be trouble, Edmund. Albany and Cornwall are bound to fight each other sooner or later." Gloucester lowered his voice. "And besides that, I had a letter from Cordelia this morning. She means to rescue her father from her sisters, and a French army has landed near Dover. If Cornwall knew about the letter, he would charge me with treason."

Edmund smiled. "Don't worry, father," he said. "Cornwall will learn nothing from me."

* * *

Outside an abandoned barn on the outskirts of Gloucester's lands, Lear stood in the lashing rain, shaking his fists at the sky. He was in the grip of a peculiar madness that made him see the truth more clearly than when he had been sane.

"Thunder and lightning, strike me down!" he raved. "I thought I was a King, but I'm a feeble old man, so useless that my own daughters don't want me!"

Kent emerged from
the barn and led
Lear inside, to
where the Fool
shivered by a
small fire.

Something
moved in the
shadows.

"Who's there?" rasped
Kent, reaching for his dagger.

"Poor Tom's cold!"
a voice screeched,
and a weird
figure leapt
into the
light. It was
Gloucester's
son, Edgar.

To escape arrest, he had dressed in rags, and smeared his face and hair with mud. If anyone spoke to him, he pretended to be mad.

"The foul fiend is after me!" Edgar whimpered.

"Poor soul!" exclaimed Lear. "Did he give everything away to his daughters, too?"

Just then,
Gloucester
ducked into
the barn,
lantern
in hand.
When
Edgar saw
his father,
he screamed,
and dashed out
into the storm.

"I must speak with the King!"
Gloucester announced.

"He wouldn't understand you, sir,"
Kent said grimly. "He has been driven out
of his mind."

"No wonder, when Goneril and Regan
are plotting against him," said Gloucester.

"His life is in danger. Take him to Dover.
The French King and his army have
landed there. Cordelia is with them."

When he heard this news, Kent felt a
glimmer of hope for Lear.

✳ ✳ ✳

Gloucester paid dearly for his loyalty to the old King. The moment he arrived back at his castle, he was seized, and brought before Cornwall and Regan, who charged him with treason. Edmund had shown Cornwall the letter from Cordelia, and had been rewarded with his father's title.

Encouraged by
Regan, Cornwall
tore out
Gloucester's
left eye. One
of Cornwall's
servants tried to
stop the torture.
He fought his
master, and was killed. Cornwall

gouged out Gloucester's
other eye, but
the Duke had
been seriously
wounded. Shortly
after Gloucester
was turned out
of his own home,
Cornwall was dead.

Gloucester spent the rest of the night wandering along country lanes, before weariness overcame him, and he sank down to sleep in a hedgerow. He was still there the following morning, when Edgar chanced upon him.

✳ ✳ ✳

Three days later, in a meadow that overlooked Dover, Lear woke to see Cordelia smiling at him. All Lear's rage had been replaced by a childlike gentleness. At first, he thought he was still asleep and dreaming, but at last he realised that Cordelia was real.

"Forgive me, I'm very old and forgetful, but aren't you my daughter?" he asked.

"I am," said Cordelia.

"I know you can't love me," Lear said, frowning. "Your sisters hate me for no reason, but you have good reason to scorn me."

"How could I scorn you?" Cordelia said gently. "You're my father. I love you as a daughter should."

She had told him so in the throne room, and he had been furious. Now Lear knew the value of her words, and he wept.

* * *

Lear's happiness was short-lived. Cordelia's husband was forced to return to France. In his absence, the English struck. The forces of Albany and Cornwall joined to drive out the invaders.

Regan and Goneril took part in the battle, and Edmund fought at Regan's side. Regan planned to marry him, and did not know that Edmund had also won Goneril's affection. He had written to her in secret, offering to marry her after she had got rid of Albany. Edmund had cleverly set the two sisters against each other.

The French were
defeated, and took
ship for France.
Lear and
Cordelia were
captured, and
sent to Edmund.

"Imprison them,
and keep a close watch on
them until their fates have been decided,"

Edmund told the
captain of the guard.
Lear was delighted.
"We'll be like
two birds in a
cage!" he said
to Cordelia.
"We'll tell tales of the
foolishness of Kings."

Edmund leaned
close to the captain.
"Take this paper,
carry out the order
written on it, and you'll
be rewarded," he promised in a whisper.

An hour later, the victors gathered.
Goneril gave Edmund a lingering look.
Regan's face was ashen, and she kept
clutching her stomach. Goneril had
poured poison into her sister's wine the
previous night, and it had begun to work.

Albany was angry. "Where are the royal prisoners, Edmund?" he demanded.

"I ordered them to be taken away," said Edmund.

"You had no right to give orders – I am in command here!" Albany growled. "Guards, fetch the prisoners."

As the guards marched off, Regan groaned, "I am sick!" and sank to her knees.

Albany ordered two soldiers to carry Regan to her tent, then he turned to Edmund. "Now the battle is over, I can turn to other matters," he said. "I know that you've been sending letters to my wife, Edmund, you filthy traitor!"

Edmund flung one of his gauntlets at Albany's feet. "No one calls me a traitor, unless he's willing to fight me to the death!" he cried.

"I will fight him, Lord Albany," someone said, and an armed stranger stepped forwards. His face was hidden under the visor of his helmet.

"Who are you?"
Edmund sneered.

"Someone
who knows that
you are a cheat
and a liar," the
stranger said.

Edmund drew his sword,
and ran at his mysterious opponent.

The fight was brutal, and brief. After
exchanging several blows, Edmund
stumbled as he tried to trip up the
stranger. He dropped
his guard, and the
edge of the
stranger's
sword bit deep
into his side.
Edmund fell.

"Save him!" shouted Goneril. She made to move towards Edmund, but Albany held her back.

"He has got what he deserved," said Albany, "and so will you, Goneril. I know you were planning to kill me, and I'm going to put you on trial for it."

"Stand trial, like a common criminal? Never!" screeched Goneril. She broke from her husband's  grasp, and rushed away before anyone could stop her.

The stranger removed his helmet, so that the dying Edmund could see him.

"Edgar!" croaked Edmund.

"Father died of a broken heart because you betrayed him," Edgar said. "Now he is avenged!"

A messenger scurried up to Albany.
"Your wife is dead, my lord!" he panted.
"She stabbed herself, and her sister Regan
died at the same instant."

A terrible cry rang out. Everybody
turned their heads, and saw Lear
approaching, carrying Cordelia's dead
body in his arms. Kent trailed behind.

"Why aren't you all howling in misery?" sobbed Lear. "Don't you understand? She's dead – she'll never come back!" He laid Cordelia down, crouched at her side, and rocked himself back and forth. "Why should a dog or a rat have life, and not you?" he whimpered.

Albany was appalled. "How did this happen?" he asked Kent.

"Edgar ordered Cordelia to be strangled,"
Kent explained. "They hanged the Fool, too."
Lear pointed at Cordelia. "Look!" he urged.
"She is breathing! She has come back to life!"

No one could bring himself to say that the old man's eyes were playing tricks on him. Lear's weary heart stopped beating, and he collapsed on Cordelia's body.

"The old have suffered most," Edmund said quietly. "I hope I won't have to suffer when I'm old."

Though nobody spoke, all who heard him shared the same hope.

I am a very foolish fond old man

Lear; IV.vii.

Chaos and Old Age in King Lear

Shakespeare wrote *King Lear* some time between 1605 and 1606. He took the story from Holinshed's *Chronicles*, and from the play *The True Chronicle History of King Leir*, which was first printed in 1605, but had been written and performed some years before.

Many people consider *King Lear* to be Shakespeare's greatest play. It tackles questions we are still asking today: what is the place of the elderly in society? Who should take care of them, and do they have a role to play?

Lear is old, and a King. Once he gives up his crown, he has no place in the world. He becomes an unwanted no one, a nothing. His vanity and rage cause him to place his trust in the daughters who least deserve it. In this, he is like Gloucester, who trusts the word of treacherous Edmund. Lear finally realises the truth when he is mad; Gloucester 'sees' the truth after he has been blinded.

When Lear divides his kingdom, chaos follows. Children turn against their parents; brothers and sisters turn against one another. Goneril plans the death of her husband, Albany. Lies are believed, and honesty is punished. Kent and Edgar are forced to disguise themselves to stay alive. During the violent storm, it seems that Nature herself has been affected.

At the end of the play, order is restored, but at a terrible cost. Rather than being defeated by the power of goodness, evil destroys itself. Lear dies, mistakenly believing that Cordelia has come back to life – a final moment of delusion that adds to the pitifulness of the tragedy.

Shakespeare and the Globe Theatre

Some of Shakespeare's most famous plays were first performed at the Globe Theatre, which was built on the South Bank of the River Thames in 1599.

Going to the Globe was a different experience from going to the theatre today. The building was roughly circular in shape, but with flat sides: a little like a doughnut crossed with a fifty-pence piece. Because the Globe was an open-air theatre, plays were only put on during daylight hours in spring and summer. People paid a penny to stand in the central space and watch a play, and this part of the audience became known as 'the groundlings' because they stood on the ground. A place in the tiers of seating beneath the thatched roof, where there was a slightly better view and less chance of being rained on, cost extra.

The Elizabethans did not bath very often and the audiences at the Globe were smelly. Fine ladies and gentlemen in the more expensive seats sniffed perfume and bags of sweetly scented herbs to cover the stink rising from the groundlings.

There were no actresses on the stage; all the female characters in Shakespeare's plays would have been acted by boys, wearing wigs and make-up. Audiences were not well behaved. People clapped and cheered when their favourite actors came on stage; bad actors were jeered at and sometimes pelted with whatever came to hand.

Most Londoners worked hard to make a living and in their precious free time they liked to be entertained. Shakespeare understood the magic of the theatre so well that today, almost four hundred years after his death, his plays still cast a spell over the thousands of people that go to see them.

Orchard Classics
Shakespeare Stories

RETOLD BY ANDREW MATTHEWS
ILLUSTRATED BY TONY ROSS

As You Like It	978 1 84616 187 2	£4.99
Hamlet	978 1 84121 340 8	£4.99
A Midsummer Night's Dream	978 1 84121 332 3	£4.99
Antony and Cleopatra	978 1 84121 338 5	£4.99
The Tempest	978 1 84121 346 0	£4.99
Richard III	978 1 84616 185 8	£4.99
Macbeth	978 1 84121 344 6	£4.99
Twelfth Night	978 1 84121 334 7	£4.99
Henry V	978 1 84121 342 2	£4.99
Romeo & Juliet	978 1 84121 336 1	£4.99
Much Ado About Nothing	978 1 84616 183 4	£4.99
Othello	978 1 84616 184 1	£4.99
Julius Caesar	978 1 40830 506 5	£4.99
King Lear	978 1 40830 503 4	£4.99
The Merchant of Venice	978 1 40830 504 1	£4.99
The Taming of the Shrew	978 1 40830 505 8	£4.99

Orchard Books are available from all good bookshops.